WARTHOGS

Katherine Walden

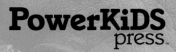

PowerKiDS press™

New York

For Molly, Kevin, and Megan Spring

Published in 2009 by The Rosen Publishing Group, Inc.
29 East 21st Street, New York, NY 10010

First Edition

Editor: Amelie von Zumbusch
Book Design: Erica Clendening
Layout Design: Julio Gil
Photo Researcher: Jessica Gerweck

Photo Credits: All images Shutterstock.com.

Library of Congress Cataloging-in-Publication Data

Walden, Katherine.
  Warthogs / Katherine Walden.— 1st ed.
      p. cm. — (Safari animals)
  Includes index.
  ISBN-13: 978-1-4358-2688-5 (library binding) — ISBN 978-1-4358-3062-2 (pbk.)
ISBN 978-1-4358-3074-5 (6-pack)
  1. Warthog—Juvenile literature. I. Title.
  QL737.U58W25 2009
  599.63'3—dc22
                                2008019531

Manufactured in the United States of America

CONTENTS

This strange-looking animal is a warthog. Warthogs are members of the pig family.

Warthogs live in Africa. They live in grasslands or open woodlands.

Warthogs have long faces.
They have big teeth
called **tusks**.

The **warts** on a warthog's face give these animals their name.

Male warthogs are known as boars. Females are sows. Babies are called piglets.

13

Sows most often have **litters** of three or four piglets. Sows take good care of their young.

A warthog family group is called a sounder. Warthog sounders eat and drink together.

Warthogs most often eat grass, fruit, and other plant parts. Sometimes, they also eat small animals.

Warthogs often **kneel** down on their front legs to dig for food.

When it is very hot,
warthogs roll in the mud.
This helps them cool off.

Words to Know

kneel

litter

tusks

wart

Index

Web Sites

Due to the changing nature of Internet links, PowerKids Press has developed an online list of Web sites related to the subject of this book. This site is updated regularly. Please use this link to access the list:
www.powerkidslinks.com/safari/warthog/